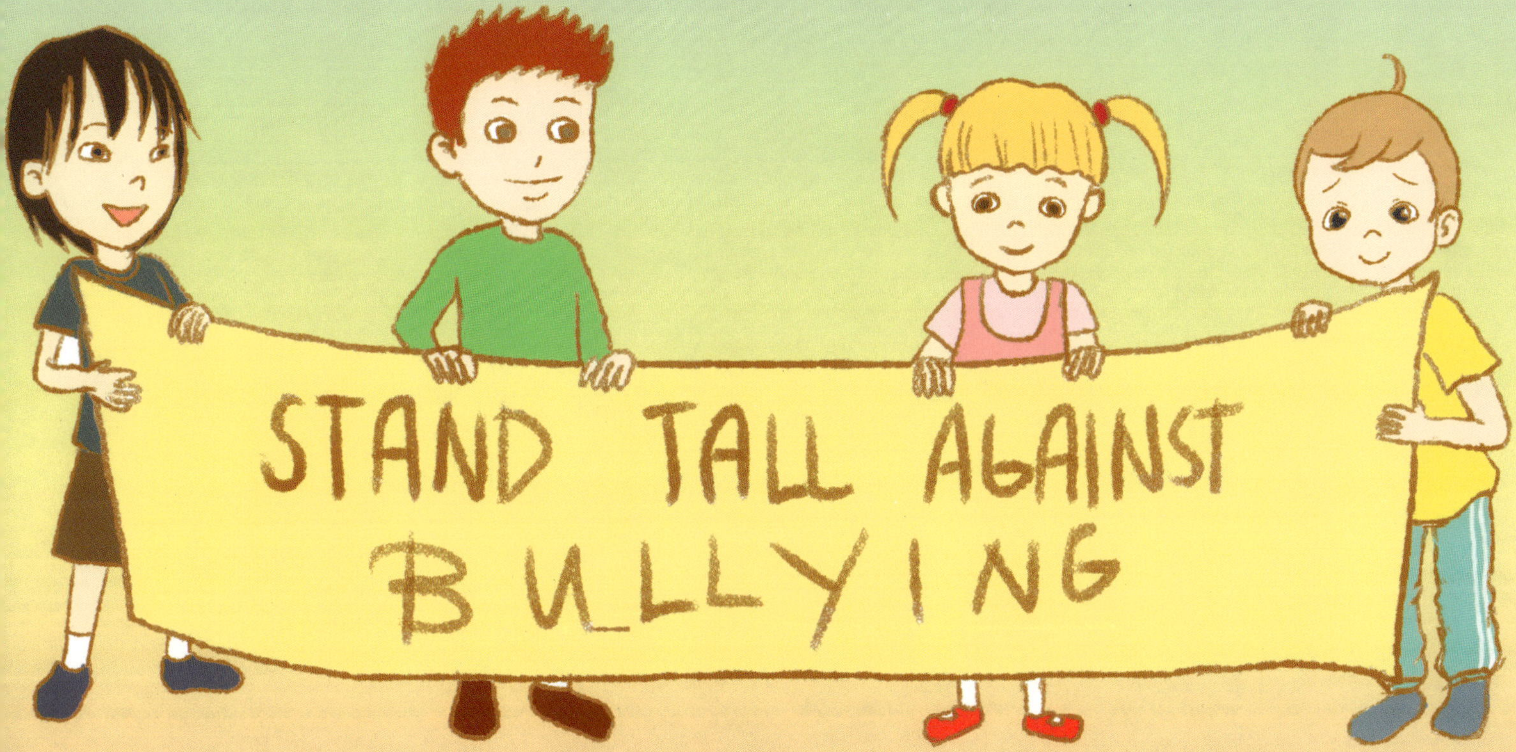
STAND TALL AGAINST
BULLYING

Copyright © 2013 by Dennis Vanasse. 133616-VANA

ISBN: Softcover   978-1-4836-3004-5
       Hardcover   978-1-4836-3005-2
       Ebook   978-1-4836-3006-9

All rights reserved. No part of this book may be reproduced or transmitted in any form or by any means, electronic or mechanical, including photocopying, recording, or by any information storage and retrieval system, without permission in writing from the copyright owner.

This is a work of fiction. Names, characters, places and incidents either are the product of the author's imagination or are used fictitiously, and any resemblance to any actual persons, living or dead, events, or locales is entirely coincidental.

Rev. date: 04/22/2013

To order additional copies of this book, contact:
Xlibris Corporation
1-888-795-4274
www.Xlibris.com
Orders@Xlibris.com

My name is Matthew, I don't know where to begin
I am eight years old and just want to fit in
I never know what its like to be cool
For many different reasons, I am afraid to go to school

This boy named BOBBY is making my life such a mess
He pushes me around when we are at recess
I can't understand why he is mean to me
I never feel good when I am around this BULLY

I avoid getting involved when my class is playing games
He makes everyone laugh by calling me names
Instead of looking at me as a special person that is unique
BOBBY imitates how I stutter whenever I speak

I hope and pray that someone will intervene
I cannot believe that BOBBY is so mean
I don't eat at school, to be hungry is not funny
The BULLY beats me up if I do not give HIM my lunch money.

I hate taking the bus, HE spits on my shirt
The BULLY gets happy when my feelings are hurt
I need help, but nobody is ever around
He grabs my books and throws them on the ground

I wish I knew what it was like to belong
HE makes me feel like I did something wrong
BOBBY tells everyone to stay away because
my clothes are smelly
When the class starts to laugh it really hurts my belly

Maybe it will just end if I start a fight
But I know that two wrongs never make a right
I get so angry, I have so much to say
The BULLY backs down if I just walk away

For BULLYING to end, it is a must
I finally have the courage to tell people I trust
First the school, who alerted my parents on the phone
Now that people know, I do not feel alone

Adults praised me for speaking out loud
I get really happy when others are proud
Hopefully, this bully will never hurt anyone again
Instead of being a foe, maybe we can be friends

I always used to think it was just a dream
To feel good and have a high self-esteem
So to all this powerful message I send
IF WE ALL STAND TOGETHER, bullying WILL END